Interactive Layer Books That Promote Reading, Writing, and Listening

Written by
Cheryl Apgar

Editor: Sheri Samoiloff
Illustrator: Darcy Tom
Cover Photographer: Michael Jarrett
Cover Illustrator: Kim Graves
Designer: Corina Chien
Cover Designer: Corina Chien
Art Director: Tom Cochrane
Project Director: Carolea Williams

Table of Contents

Introduction

Layer It! Each Month brings the love of reading and writing into the early-childhood classroom. This innovative resource shows you how to help each child in your class create one thematic, interactive, rhyming layer book for each month of the year. Easy-to-follow directions, lively illustrations, and moveable art pieces make these twelve books fun for teachers and children alike!

A child's language skills develop quickly during the early-childhood years. Children develop their listening skills, increase their vocabulary, and begin to make the transition from oral to written language. *Layer It! Each Month* provides the materials for reinforcing these skills. Children practice their fine motor skills as they color, cut out, and organize their very own layer books. The completed books become great tools for shared and independent reading and enhance any unit of study.

Children can construct these layer books with minimal or no help from an adult, making them a great tool for building a child's independence and self-esteem. Very little teacher preparation is involved, and all suggested materials can be substituted with other materials. In addition, each layer book includes a writing prompt to help children explore the connections between the theme of study and their own life.

Each layer of these adorable, hands-on books brings a year's worth of opportunities for children to grow as readers, writers, speakers, and listeners!

# Making a Layer Book

The construction of each layer book is a progressive, week-long activity. Children complete one page each day, allowing for daily review of concepts and reinforcement of targeted skills. (See the activity ideas on pages 6–8.) Essentially, each layer book is a theme-related poem with corresponding art pieces that children color, cut out, and glue on the four pages of the book.

Each layer book includes a directions page that consists of a materials list and a detailed explanation of how to create each layer book page; a reproducible page of art pieces; and four reproducible layer book pages. Follow these step-by-step directions to guide children through the creation of each layer book:

1. Write each child's name on a separate file folder. Have children title the folder *Layer Books in Progress*.

2. Copy all the reproducibles shown in the materials list on 9" x 12" (23 cm x 30.5 cm) pieces of construction paper. Use the recommended colors listed in the materials list, or select your own colors.

3. Give each child the reproducible page of art pieces and an envelope. Have children color and cut out the art pieces and then store them in their envelope. Ask children to write their name on their envelope. Have them place their envelope in their file folder.

4. Decide whether you want children to assemble each book from front to back or back to front. If children start with page 1, they will read each line of the poem as they assemble their book. If they start with page 4, they can easily stack their completed pages in the correct order. Choose the method that works best with your class.

5. At the beginning of each day's activity, give children their file folder, a reproducible page, and the necessary art materials for that page. Use the directions page to show children how to cut off the diamond pattern on the reproducible, how to color and/or use art materials to decorate the remainder of the page, and where to glue each art piece. At the end of each day's activity, have children place their envelope and their completed page in their folder. Collect the folders.

6. You will need to cut a slit in one or more pages of each layer book. The directions page indicates exactly where to make each slit. Use an X-ACTO® knife or a sharp pair of scissors to cut the slit in each child's copy of the page before he or she works with it. Never allow children to handle X-ACTO® knives or sharp scissors.

7. Children will need at least one craft stick for most of the layer books. Cut craft sticks as needed to fit a page. For example, if the directions call for a craft stick to be used on page 1 or 2 of a book, cut the sticks to make them shorter (so that they do not obstruct pages 3 and 4). Have children glue the center of the art piece on the stick in a horizontal or vertical direction depending on the page setup. You can substitute straws, coffee stirrers, cut index cards, or other sturdy items for craft sticks.

8. Once children have completed all the pages of their book, make sure their pages are in sequential order. Staple together the completed books, and have a reading celebration.

9. Invite children to read their completed book in a whole-class setting or during guided reading, partner reading, or independent reading. Have them read their book chorally, or assign each child a page to read for a reader's theater.

Skill Building

Before the class begins to assemble a layer book, use the ideas in this section to introduce the theme and prepare children to read the text. Then, after children have assembled and explored their book, choose one of the assessment tools to determine their mastery of reading and writing skills. Choose additional skill-building activities that complement your unit of study. All activities are flexible, and you can alter the directions to fit the needs of your class.

Before You Begin

Before you introduce a layer book, ask children to share what they know about the theme. Write children's ideas on a piece of chart paper, and display it on a board or wall.

Introducing the Theme

Use the following ideas to introduce the theme of study:

- Read aloud books about the theme.

- Have children make murals about the theme. Label the items in the murals that relate to the theme.

- Make a thematic word wall or class dictionary of thematic terms.

- Write thematic words on die-cut shapes or stationery, and display them around the room.

Presenting the Layer Book

Each time you select a layer book for children to complete, use the following activities throughout the week to teach new concepts and reinforce skills. Introduce one or two skills each day.

Analyze This ••

Write the poem from the chosen layer book on a large piece of chart paper or sentence strips. Display the chart paper, or place the sentence strips in a pocket chart. Use a different color ink for each line of the poem. As an option, laminate the chart paper so you can write on it with overhead transparency markers. Use a wet paper towel to wipe off the ink at the end of each activity.

- Introduce the selected poem by asking children to read it (as they are able) and look for familiar words. Engage children in conversation about the subject to assess their prior knowledge and to introduce the concept.

- Point to each word, and have children echo each line of the poem as you read it. Emphasize rhyming words by underlining each rime on the chart.

- Say or sing the poem as you point to the words on the chart. Invite volunteers to point to the words on the chart while the rest of the class reads along.

- Have children search for capital letters. Invite children to circle each capital letter.

- Have children search for punctuation marks. Invite children to draw a triangle around each punctuation mark. Discuss the name of each mark.

- Invite children to identify and spell all the rhyming words.

- Challenge advanced children to use the rimes to make a list of other rhyming words and then substitute the new words to make a nonsense poem.

- Invite children to use simple instruments or jump ropes as they sing or chant the poem.

- Write five high-frequency words on the chalkboard. Have children search through their completed layer book to see how many of the high-frequency words from the board are also in their book. As a class, read the high-frequency words found in the layer book.

Extension Activities

Use the following activities to have children practice their listening skills, locate punctuation marks, review parts of speech, learn rhyming words, and practice letter recognition.

Are You Listening? •

Alter the sentences to fit each layer book. Have children set their completed book in front of them before you begin. Slowly read aloud the directions, and pause after each direction.

1. Point to the_____ on page _____ of your book.
2. Find the object in your book that you can slide. Whisper the name of the object.
3. Draw a _____ on page 4.
4. Count the number of feet you can find in your book.
5. Count the number of eyes you can find in your book.
6. Find your favorite page. Draw a happy face on the back of the page.
7. Find the last page in your book. Read that page silently.
8. Count the number of capital letters in your book. Hold up the same number of fingers as your answer.
9. Lift the flap on page _____. What do you see? Stand up if you see an animal.
10. Are there two or more children in your book? If yes, raise your index finger.

Assess children's listening skills by observing their actions, their interactions with others, and their answers.

Show Me •

Begin by writing the poem on a piece of chart paper, or have children follow along in their completed layer book. Customize the directions to correspond to the poem in each layer book.

Ask children to place their index finger on the following:
- a specific capital letter
- a vowel
- a consonant
- a word that begins with the same letter as the first letter in their first name
- a word that ends with the same letter as the first letter in their last name
- a word that rhymes with _____

September: School Is Cool

Materials

- Art Pieces reproducible (page 10) white
- Page One reproducible (page 11) light brown
- Page Two reproducible (page 12) light green
- Page Three reproducible (page 13) yellow
- Page Four reproducible (page 14) pink
- crayons or markers
- scissors
- X-ACTO® knife (optional) (for teacher use only)
- craft sticks
- glue
- cotton balls

Directions

Art Pieces Give each child an Art Pieces reproducible and an envelope. Have children color and cut out the six art pieces and place them inside their envelope. Tell children to place their envelope in their file folder. Collect each child's folder, and distribute it at the beginning of each day's activity.

Page One Cut a slit next to the letter A on each child's Page One reproducible. Give children their revised page and a craft stick.

Have children remove the school bus art piece from their envelope and glue it to the craft stick. Tell children to cut off the diamond pattern on the page and discard it. Ask them to color the remainder of the page and then slide the prepared craft stick through the slit.

Page Two Give each child a Page Two reproducible, and have children remove the kids art piece from their envelope. Tell children to cut off the diamond pattern on the page and discard it. Ask them to color the remainder of the page and glue the kids over the letter B.

Page Three Give each child a Page Three reproducible, and have children remove the backpacks, lunch boxes, and pencils art pieces from their envelope. Tell children to cut off the diamond pattern on the page and discard it. Ask them to color the remainder of the page and glue the backpacks over the letter C, the lunch boxes over the letter D, and the pencils over the letter E.

Page Four Give each child a Page Four reproducible and one cotton ball. Have children remove the door art piece from their envelope. Ask children to draw a picture of themselves in the doorway. Have them glue the left edge of the door over the letter F (along the left edge of the doorway) and then color the remainder of the page. Have children tear their cotton ball into small pieces and glue the pieces over the clouds. Invite children to respond to the writing prompt. Set aside the pages until the glue is dry.

Art Pieces

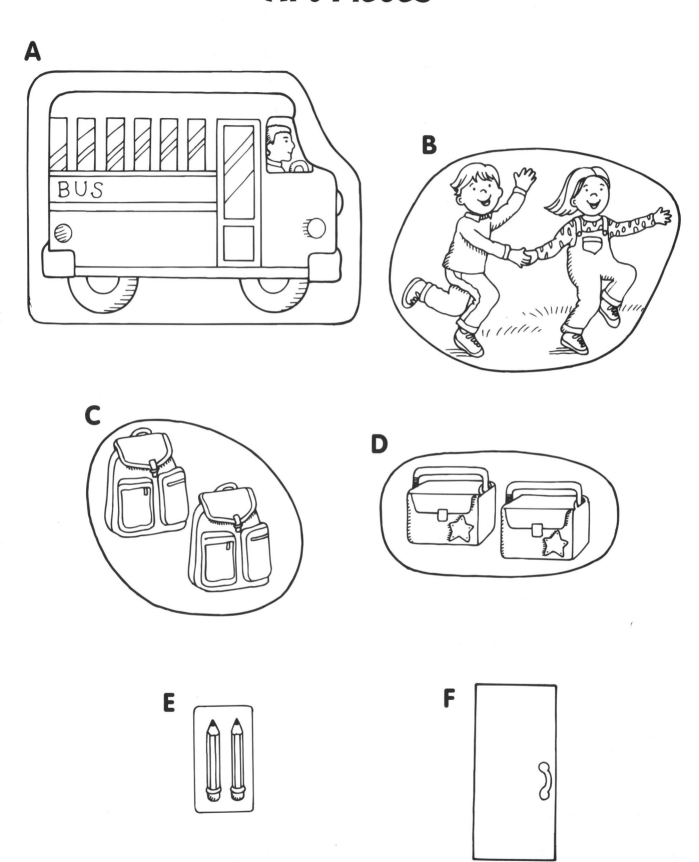

A

B

C

D

E

F

Layer It! Each Month © 2002 Creative Teaching Press

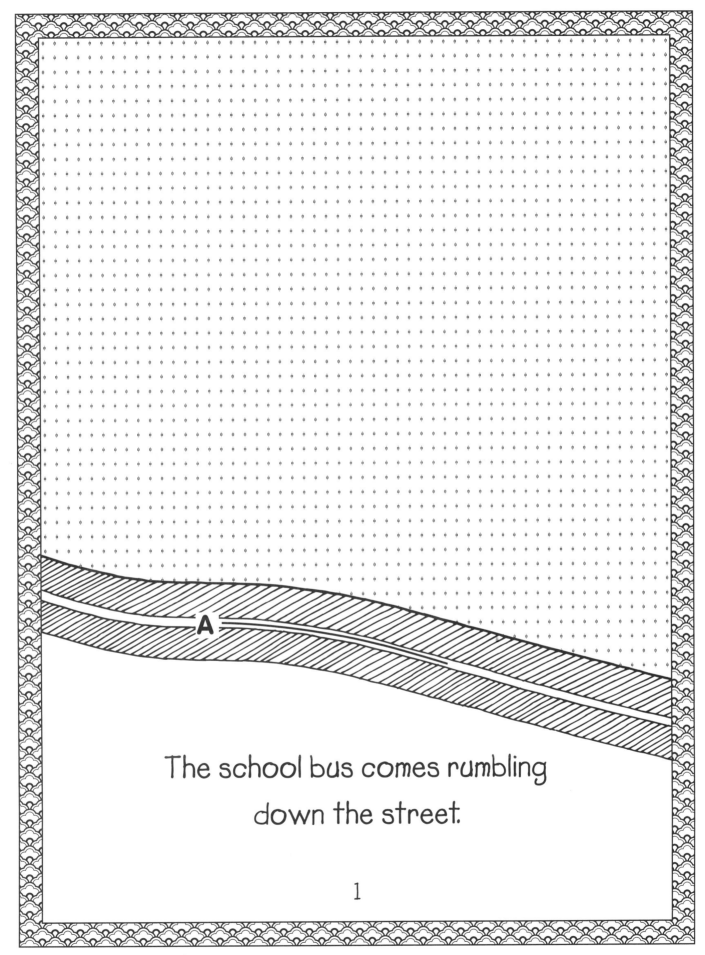

The school bus comes rumbling down the street.

1

B

Children are running
with skip-hoppity feet.

2

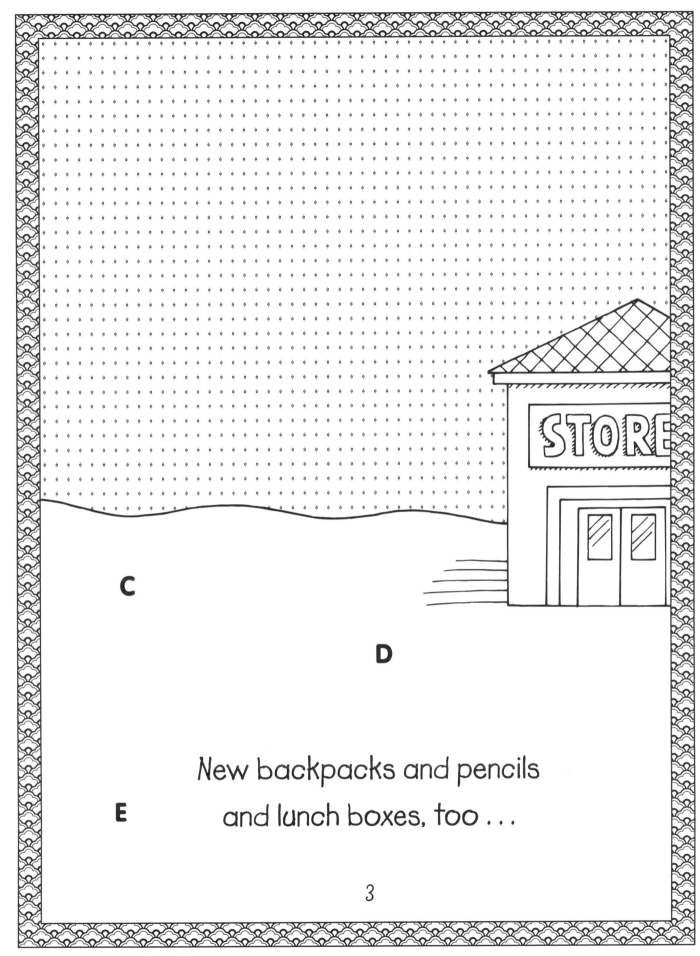

C

D

E

New backpacks and pencils
and lunch boxes, too . . .

3

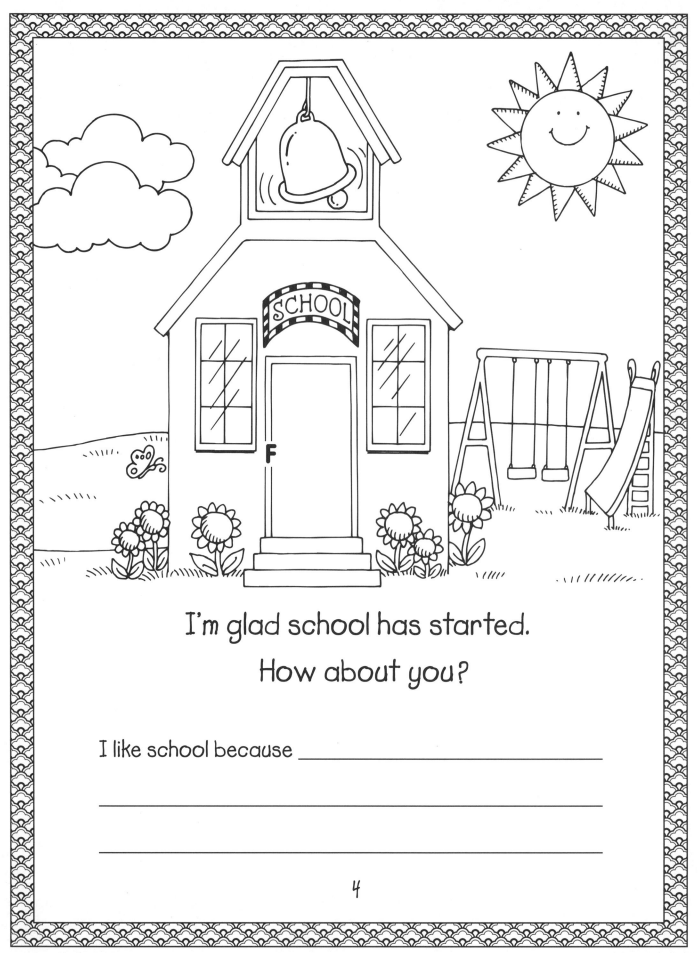

I'm glad school has started.

How about you?

I like school because _____

_____

_____

4

October: Autumn Fun

Materials

- ✄ Art Pieces reproducible (page 16) white
- ✄ Page One reproducible (page 17) light green
- ✄ Page Two reproducible (page 18) green
- ✄ Page Three reproducible (page 19) light brown
- ✄ Page Four reproducible (page 20) light blue
- ✄ crayons or markers
- ✄ scissors
- ✄ gold and green glitter
- ✄ glue
- ✄ X-ACTO® knife (optional) (for teacher use only)
- ✄ craft sticks
- ✄ cotton balls

Directions •

Art Pieces Give each child an Art Pieces reproducible and an envelope. Have children color and cut out the six art pieces and place them inside their envelope. Tell children to place their envelope in their file folder. Collect each child's folder, and distribute it at the beginning of each day's activity.

Page One Give each child a Page One reproducible and gold and green glitter. Tell children to cut off the diamond pattern on the page and discard it. Ask them to color the remainder of the page and glue glitter on the leaves. Set aside the pages until the glue is dry.

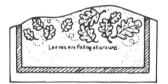

Page Two Cut a slit next to the letter A on each child's Page Two reproducible. Give children their revised page and a craft stick. Have them remove the squirrels art piece from their envelope and glue it to the craft stick. Tell children to cut off the diamond pattern on the page and discard it. Ask them to color the remainder of the page and then slide the prepared craft stick through the slit.

Page Three Give each child a Page Three reproducible, and have children remove the horse and barn door art pieces from their envelope. Tell children to cut off the diamond pattern on the page and discard it. Ask them to color the remainder of the page and glue the horse over the letter B. Have them glue the left edge of the barn door over the letter C (along the left edge of the doorway).

Page Four Give each child a Page Four reproducible and one cotton ball. Have children remove the cloud, squirrel, and birds art pieces from their envelope. Invite them to tear their cotton ball into small pieces and glue the pieces to the cloud art piece. Set aside the art pieces until the glue is dry. Have children color the page and then glue the cloud over the letter D, the squirrel over the letter E, and the birds over the letter F. Invite them to respond to the writing prompt.

Art Pieces

A

B

C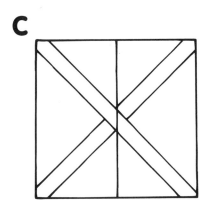

D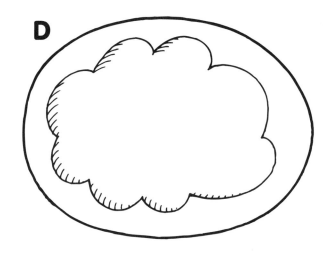

E

F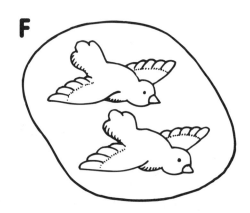

Leaves are falling all around.

1

Layer It! Each Month © 2002 Creative Teaching Press

A ————————————

Squirrels gather nuts
that have fallen to the ground.

2

The harvest is in.
There's a chill in the air.

3

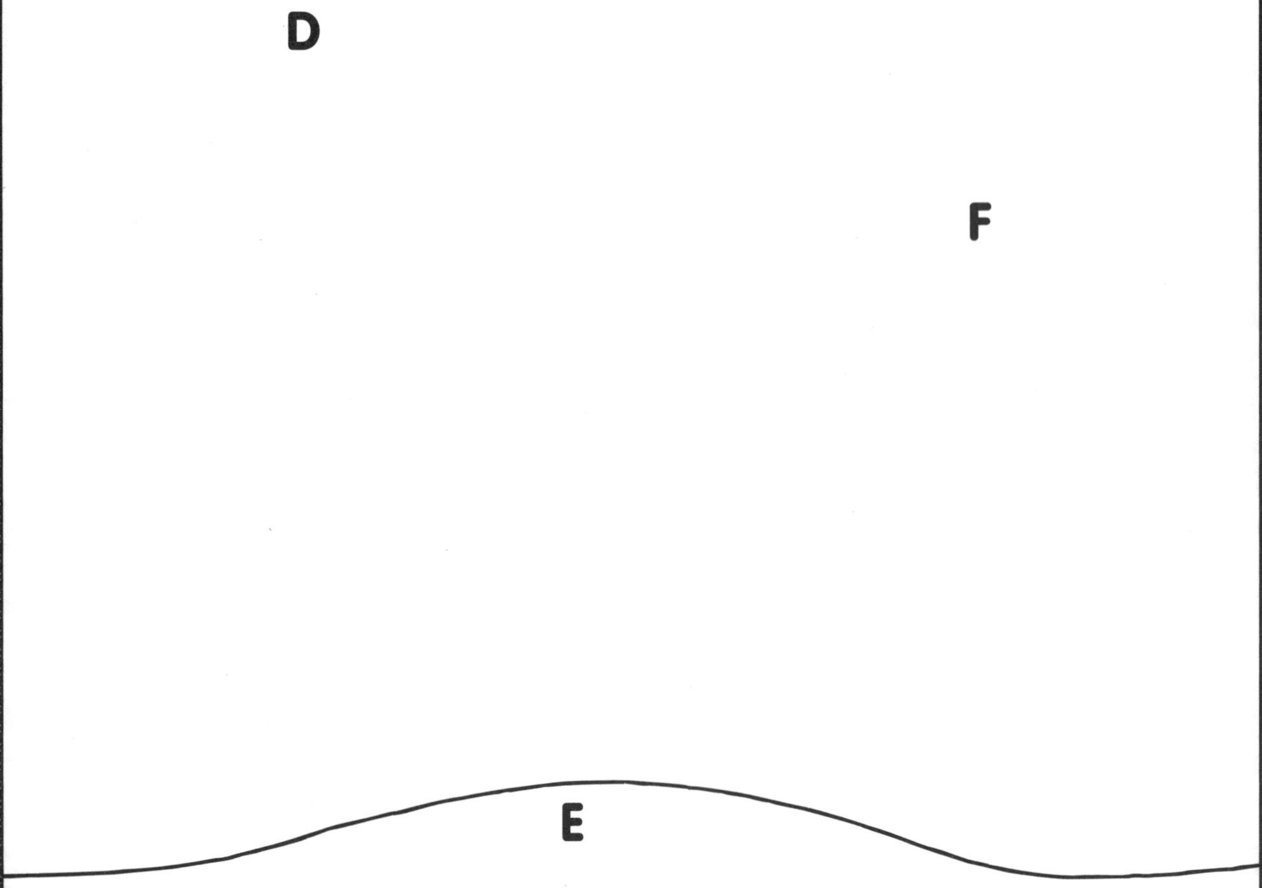

D

F

E

There are signs of autumn
everywhere.

My favorite thing to do in autumn is _____

_____

_____

4

november: The Pilgrims' New Life

Materials

- ✂ Art Pieces reproducible (page 22) white
- ✂ Page One reproducible (page 23) blue
- ✂ Page Two reproducible (page 24) tan
- ✂ Page Three reproducible (page 25) green
- ✂ Page Four reproducible (page 26) light blue
- ✂ crayons or markers
- ✂ scissors
- ✂ X-ACTO® knife (optional) (for teacher use only)
- ✂ craft sticks
- ✂ glue
- ✂ translucent glitter
- ✂ seeds (e.g., sunflower seeds, pumpkin seeds)

The Pilgrims came from England, far across the sea.

Directions

Art Pieces Give each child an Art Pieces reproducible and an envelope. Have children color and cut out the five art pieces and place them inside their envelope. Tell children to place their envelope in their file folder. Collect each child's folder, and distribute it at the beginning of each day's activity.

Page One Cut a slit next to the letter A on each child's Page One reproducible. Give children their revised page and a craft stick. Have them remove the Mayflower ship art piece from their envelope and glue it to the craft stick. Tell children to cut off the diamond pattern on the page and discard it. Ask them to color the remainder of the page and then slide the prepared craft stick through the slit.

The Pilgrims came from England, far across the sea.

Page Two Give each child a Page Two reproducible. Have children remove the Pilgrim man and Pilgrim woman art pieces from their envelope. Tell children to cut off the diamond pattern on the page and discard it. Ask them to color the remainder of the page and then glue the Pilgrim man over the letter B and the Pilgrim woman over the letter C.

Their life was hard, but they were brave and happy to be free.

Page Three Give each child a Page Three reproducible and a handful of seeds. Have children remove the Pilgrim and Native American men art piece from their envelope. Tell children to cut off the diamond pattern on the page and discard it. Ask them to color the remainder of the page and glue the seeds around the corn stalks. Have children glue the Pilgrim and Native American men over the letter D. Set aside the pages until the glue is dry.

They were welcomed by the natives who taught them many things.

Page Four Give each child a Page Four reproducible and translucent glitter. Have children remove the door art piece from their envelope. Invite them to draw in the doorway of the house a Pilgrim man, woman, or child carrying a treat for the feast. Ask children to color the remainder of the page. Have them glue the left edge of the door over the letter E (along the left edge of the doorway). Invite children to respond to the writing prompt and then glue glitter on the mountain peaks to resemble snow. Set aside the pages until the glue is dry.

Then they gathered together for the feast we call Thanksgiving.

I am thankful for my family and friends.

Art Pieces

A

B

C

D

E

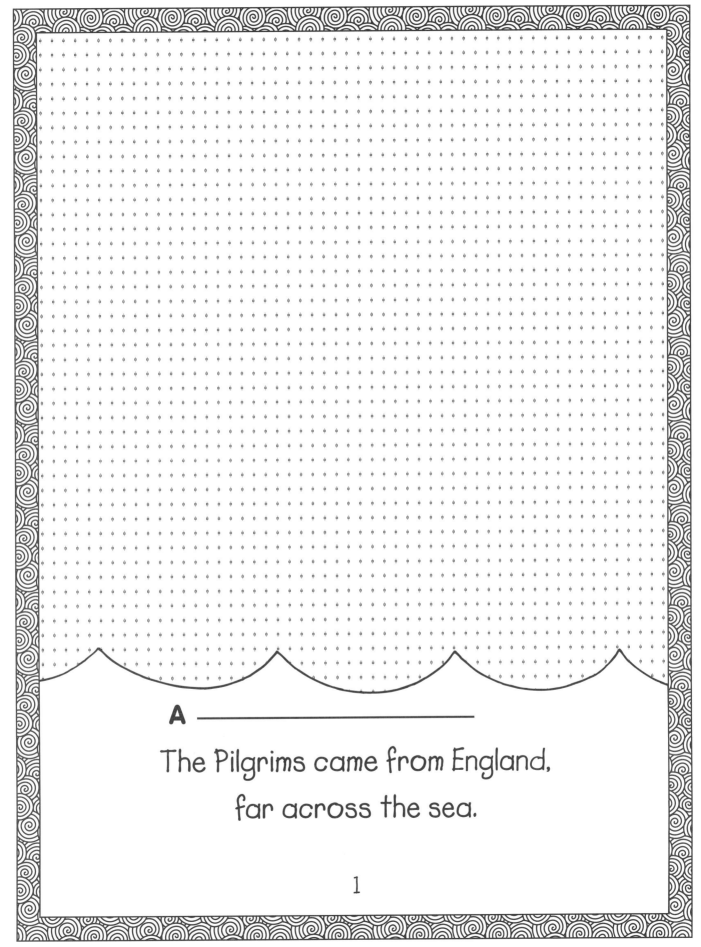

A —————————

The Pilgrims came from England,
far across the sea.

1

C z

B

Their life was hard,
but they were brave
and happy to be free.

2

D

They were welcomed by the natives
who taught them many things.

3

Then they gathered together for the feast
we call Thanksgiving.

I am thankful for _____

_____

_____

4

December: Let's Celebrate

Materials

- ✂ Art Pieces reproducible (page 28) white
- ✂ Page One reproducible (page 29) tan
- ✂ Page Two reproducible (page 30) yellow
- ✂ Page Three reproducible (page 31) light green
- ✂ Page Four reproducible (page 32) light blue
- ✂ crayons or markers
- ✂ scissors
- ✂ gold, silver, and red glitter
- ✂ glue
- ✂ X-ACTO® knife (optional) (for teacher use only)
- ✂ craft sticks
- ✂ brass fasteners

Directions •

Art Pieces Give each child an Art Pieces reproducible and an envelope. Have children color and cut out the six art pieces and place them inside their envelope. Tell children to place their envelope in their file folder. Collect each child's folder, and distribute it at the beginning of each day's activity.

Page One Give each child a Page One reproducible and gold glitter. Have children remove the Menorah and Kinara art pieces from their envelope. Tell children to cut off the diamond pattern on the page and discard it. Ask them to color the remainder of the page and then glue the Menorah over the letter A and the Kinara over the letter B. Have children glue glitter on the flames of each candle. Set aside the pages until the glue is dry.

Page Two Cut a slit next to the letter D on each child's Page Two reproducible. Give children their revised page and a craft stick. Have children remove the piñata and girl art pieces from their envelope. Tell children to cut off the diamond pattern on the page and discard it.

Ask them to color the remainder of the page. Have children glue the girl to the craft stick, glue the piñata over the letter C, and slide the prepared craft stick through the slit.

Page Three Give each child a Page Three reproducible and gold, silver, and red glitter. Have children remove the stockings art piece from their envelope. Tell children to cut off the diamond pattern on the page and discard it. Ask them to color the remainder of the page, glue the stockings over the letter E, and glue glitter on the Christmas tree ornaments. Set aside the pages until the glue is dry.

Page Four Give each child a Page Four reproducible and a brass fastener. Have children remove the world art piece from their envelope. Ask them to color the page and then place the brass fastener through the dot on the world and the dot on the page (below the letter F). Invite children to respond to the writing prompt.

Art Pieces

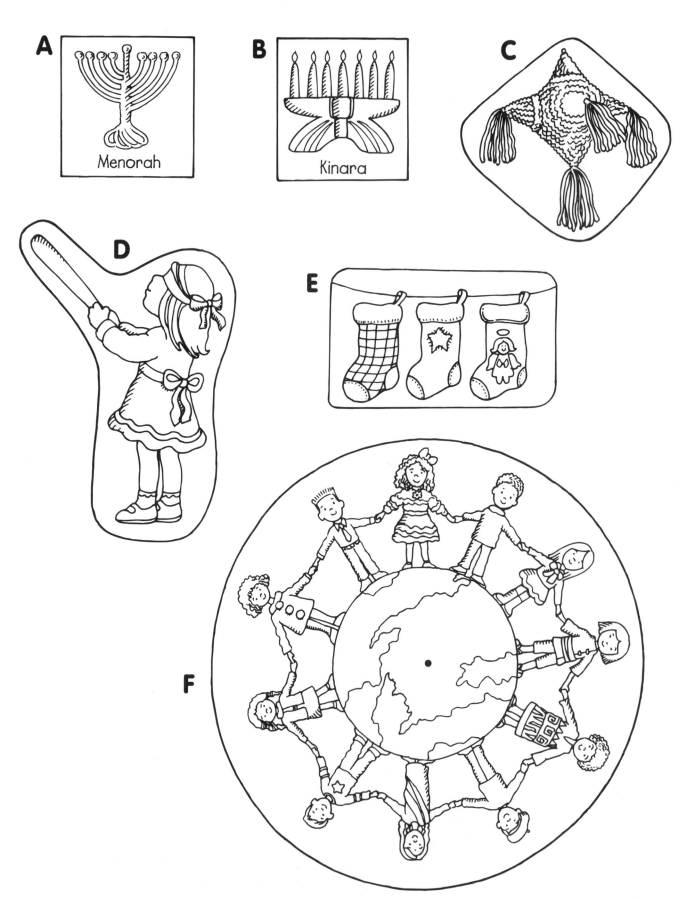

A Menorah

B Kinara

C

D

E

F

Layer It! Each Month © 2002 Creative Teaching Press

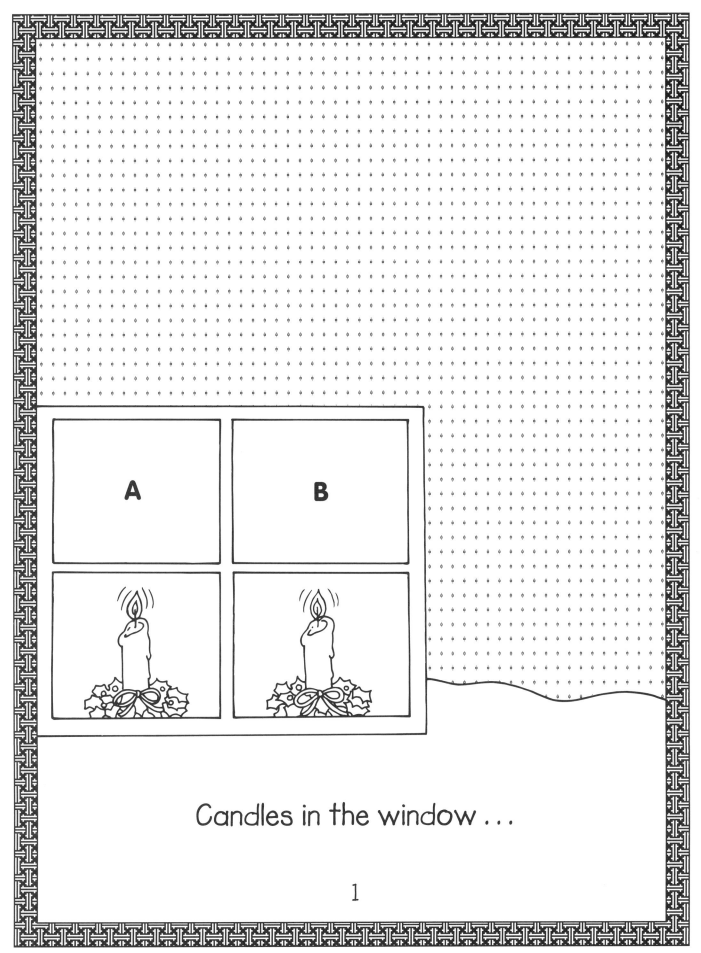

Candles in the window . . .

1

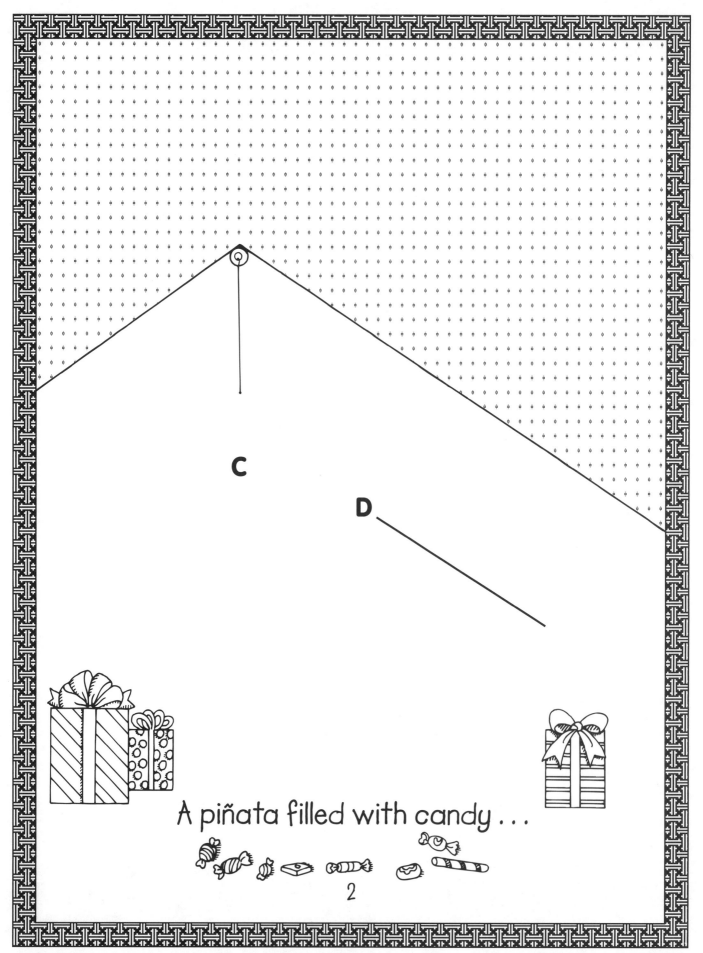

C

D

A piñata filled with candy . . .

2

Stockings by the fireplace . . .

3

Happy Holidays

F
•

The holidays are dandy.

I will give a special gift to _____ because

_____

_____

4

Layer It! Each Month © 2002 Creative Teaching Press

January: Winter Wonderland

Materials

- ✂ Art Pieces reproducible (page 34) white
- ✂ Page One reproducible (page 35) white
- ✂ Page Two reproducible (page 36) white
- ✂ Page Three reproducible (page 37) white
- ✂ Page Four reproducible (page 38) white
- ✂ crayons or markers
- ✂ scissors
- ✂ translucent glitter
- ✂ glue
- ✂ X-ACTO® knife (optional) (for teacher use only)
- ✂ craft sticks

Directions •

Art Pieces Give each child an Art Pieces reproducible and an envelope. Have children color and cut out the six art pieces and place them inside their envelope. Tell children to place their envelope in their file folder. Collect each child's folder, and distribute it at the beginning of each day's activity.

Page One Give each child a Page One reproducible and translucent glitter. Tell children to cut off the diamond pattern on the page and discard it. Ask them to color the remainder of the page to resemble wind and snow and then glue glitter around the page to resemble snow. Set aside the pages until the glue is dry.

Page Two Give each child a Page Two reproducible. Have children remove the squirrel, bear, and two cover art pieces from their envelope. Tell children to cut off the diamond pattern on the page and discard it. Ask them to color the remainder of the page to resemble wind and snow. Invite children to glue the squirrel over the letter A and the bear over the letter B. Have them glue the top edge of the small cover over the letter C (along the top edge of the

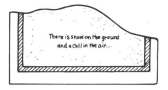

small cave) and glue the top edge of the large cover over the letter D (along the top edge of the large cave).

Page Three Cut a slit next to the letter E on each child's Page Three reproducible. Give children their revised page and a craft stick. Have them remove the child art piece from their envelope and glue it to the craft stick. Tell children to cut off the diamond pattern on the page and discard it. Ask them to color the remainder of the page to resemble wind and snow, and invite them to slide the prepared craft stick through the slit.

Page Four Give each child a Page Four reproducible and translucent glitter. Have children remove the snowman art piece from their envelope. Ask them to color the page and glue the snowman over the letter F. Invite children to respond to the writing prompt and then glue glitter on the tree and ground to resemble snow. Set aside the pages until the glue is dry.

Art Pieces

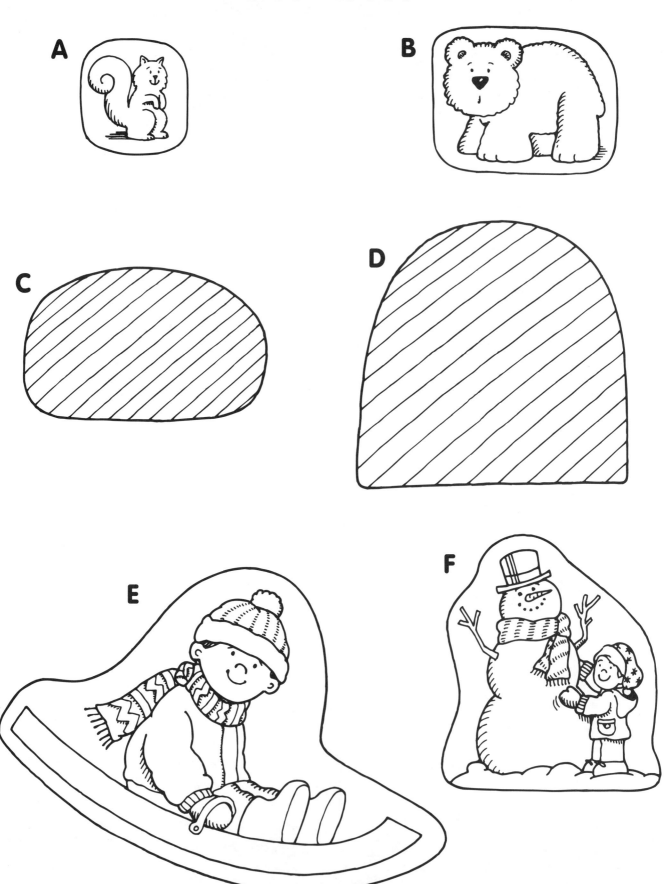

A

B

C

D

E

F

Layer It! Each Month © 2002 Creative Teaching Press

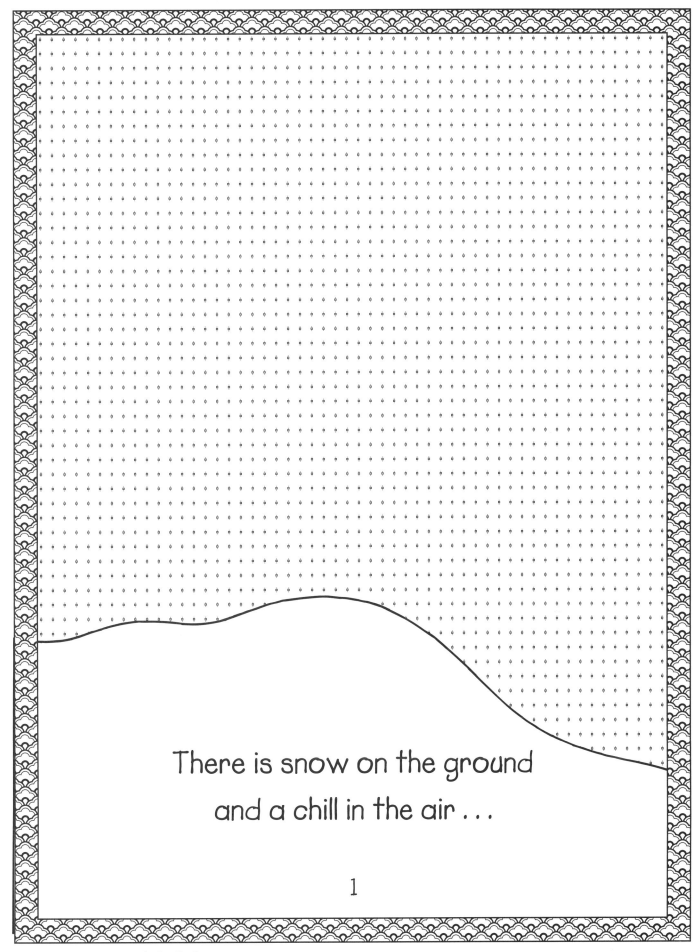

There is snow on the ground
and a chill in the air . . .

1

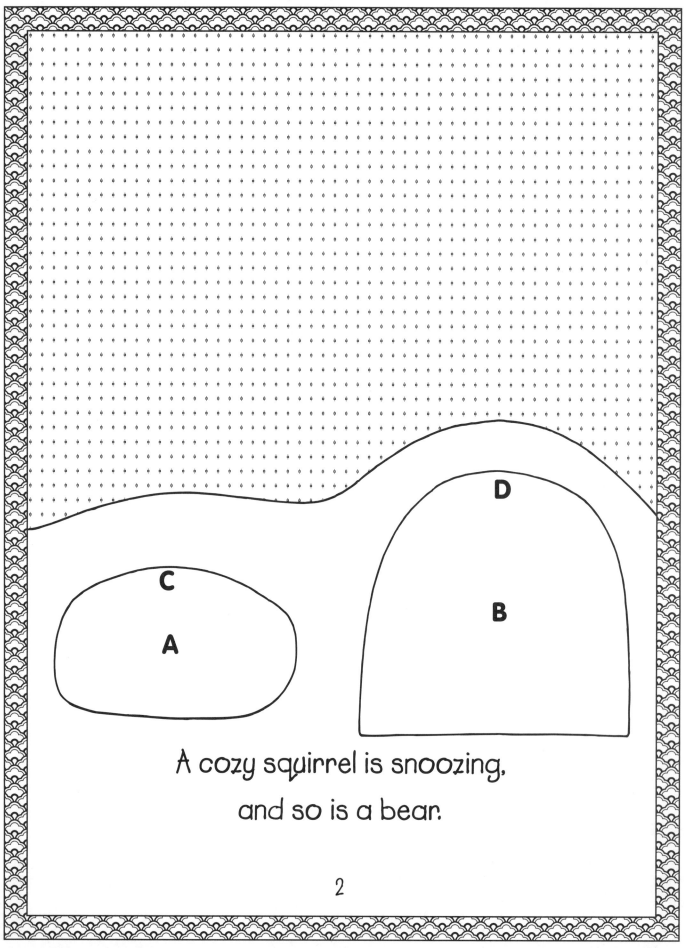

A cozy squirrel is snoozing,
and so is a bear.

2

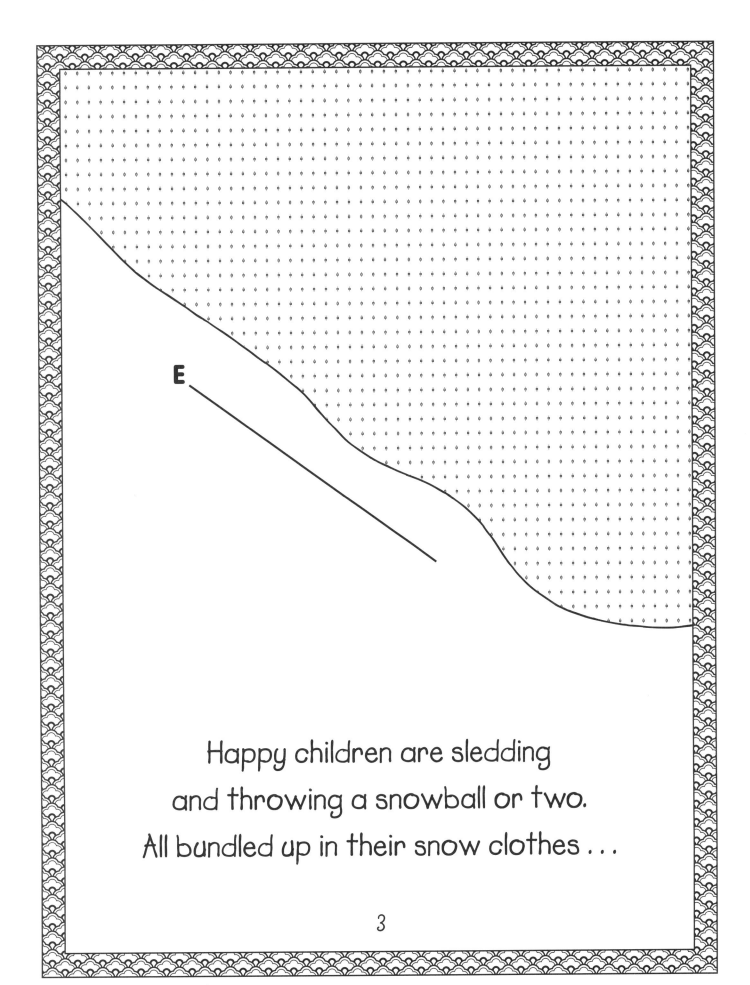

Happy children are sledding
and throwing a snowball or two.
All bundled up in their snow clothes . . .

3

F

They like winter, don't you?

I like winter because _____

_____

_____

4

February: Lace and Hearts

Materials

- ✂ Art Pieces reproducible (page 40) white
- ✂ Page One reproducible (page 41) pink
- ✂ Page Two reproducible (page 42) white
- ✂ Page Three reproducible (page 43) lavender
- ✂ Page Four reproducible (page 44) red or white
- ✂ crayons or markers
- ✂ scissors
- ✂ real lace (optional)
- ✂ glue
- ✂ red glitter
- ✂ 1" (2.5 cm) scrap paper squares

Directions

Art Pieces Give each child an Art Pieces reproducible and an envelope. Have children color and cut out the seven art pieces and place them inside their envelope. Tell children to place their envelope in their file folder. Collect each child's folder, and distribute it at the beginning of each day's activity.

Page One Give each child a Page One reproducible and a piece of real lace. Have children remove the paper scraps and lace art pieces from their envelope. Tell them to cut off the diamond pattern on the page and discard it. Invite children to glue the paper scraps over the letter A and the paper lace over the letter B. Ask them to glue the piece of real lace around the page. Set aside the pages until the glue is dry.

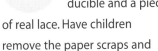

Page Two Give each child a Page Two reproducible and red glitter. Have children remove the lace heart and the shaded heart art pieces from their envelope. Tell children to cut off the diamond pattern on the page and discard it. Ask them to color the remainder of the page and glue the lace heart over the letter C and the shaded heart over the letter D. Have children glue glitter on the large heart. Set aside the pages until the glue is dry.

Page Three Give each child a Page Three reproducible and two scrap paper squares. Have children remove the note and double hearts art pieces from their envelope. Tell children to cut off the diamond pattern on the page and discard it. Ask them to color the remainder of the page. Have children fold the two scrap paper squares "accordion style." Show them how to glue each art piece onto one end of a folded paper square. Then, have children glue over the letter E the opposite end of the folded paper with the note on it. Have them glue over the letter F the opposite end of the folded paper with the double hearts on it. The art pieces should "pop off" the page. Set aside the pages until the glue is dry.

Page Four Give each child a Page Four reproducible. Have children remove the large heart art piece from their envelope. Ask them to color the page and then glue the top edge of the heart over the letter G (along the top edge of the I Love You! sign). Invite children to respond to the writing prompt.

Art Pieces

A

B

D

C

F

E

You are
a very
special
person.

G

Layer It! Each Month © 2002 Creative Teaching Press

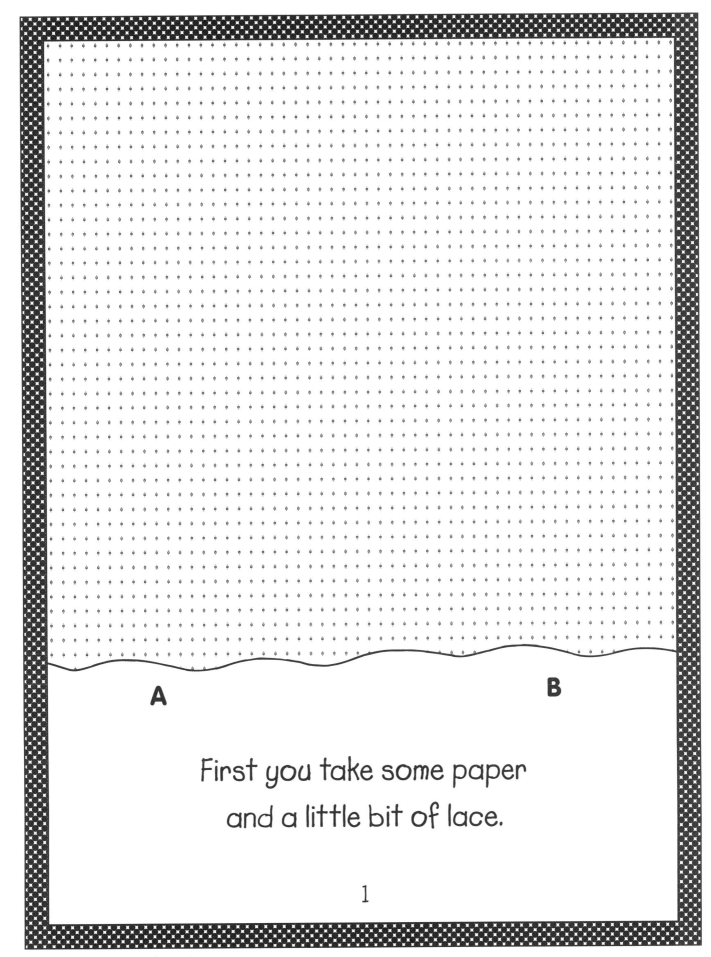

A

B

First you take some paper
and a little bit of lace.

1

C

D

Then cut and snip the heart a bit,
and put it all in place.

2

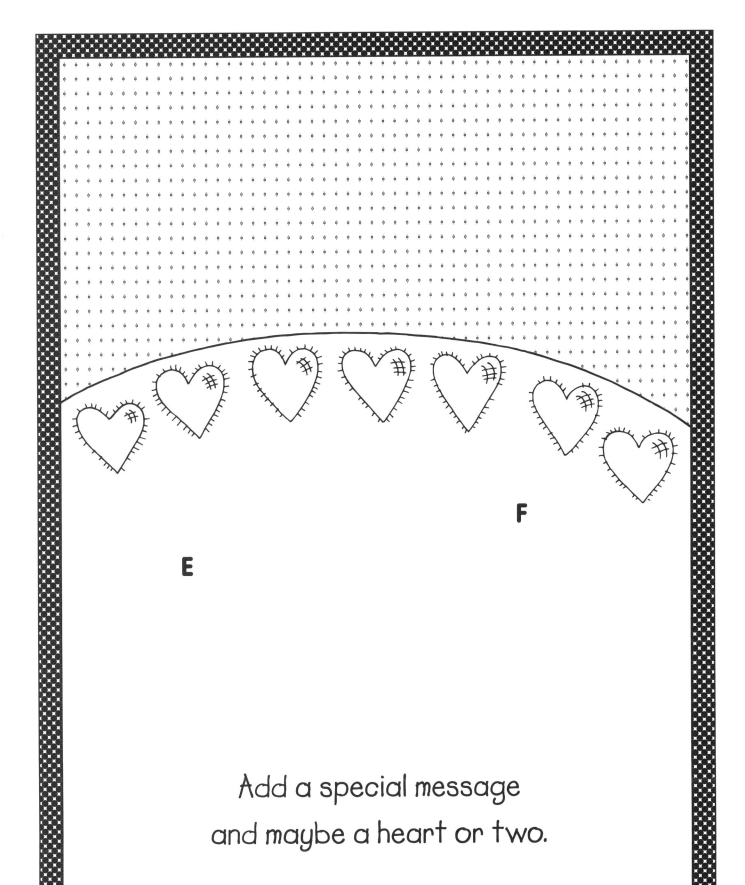

E

F

Add a special message
and maybe a heart or two.

3

G

I Love You!

So when this is opened,
your friend will read . . .

I love you because _____

_____

_____

4

March: Lucky Leprechauns

Materials

- ✂ Art Pieces reproducible (page 46) white
- ✂ Page One reproducible (page 47) light green
- ✂ Page Two reproducible (page 48) green
- ✂ Page Three reproducible (page 49) tan
- ✂ Page Four reproducible (page 50) white
- ✂ crayons or markers
- ✂ scissors
- ✂ green, gold, and translucent glitter
- ✂ glue
- ✂ X-ACTO® knife (optional) (for teacher use only)
- ✂ craft sticks
- ✂ watercolor paint/paintbrushes
- ✂ cups of water

Directions •

Art Pieces Give each child an Art Pieces reproducible and an envelope. Have children color and cut out the four art pieces and place them inside their envelope. Tell children to place their envelope in their file folder. Collect each child's folder, and distribute it at the beginning of each day's activity.

Page One Give each child a Page One reproducible and green glitter. Tell children to cut off the diamond pattern on the page and discard it. Ask them to color the remainder of the page and glue glitter on the shamrocks. Set aside the pages until the glue is dry.

Page Two Give each child a Page Two reproducible and gold glitter. Have children remove the pot of gold art piece from their envelope. Tell children to cut off the diamond pattern on the page and discard it. Ask them to color the remainder of the page, glue the pot of gold over the letter A, and glue glitter on the coins. Set aside the pages until the glue is dry.

Page Three Cut a slit next to the letter B on each child's Page Three reproducible. Give children their revised page and a craft stick. Have them remove the leprechaun art piece from their envelope and glue it to the craft stick. Tell children to cut off the diamond pattern on the page and discard it. Ask them to color the remainder of the page. Invite children to respond to the writing prompt and then slide the prepared craft stick through the slit.

Page Four Give each child a Page Four reproducible, paint and a paintbrush, a cup of water, and translucent glitter. Invite children to paint the sky on their paper. Set aside the pages until the paint is dry. Have children remove the sun and rainbow art pieces from their envelope. Invite children to glue glitter over the rainbow. Set aside the art pieces until the glue is dry. Have children glue the sun over the letter C and the rainbow over the letter D.

Art Pieces

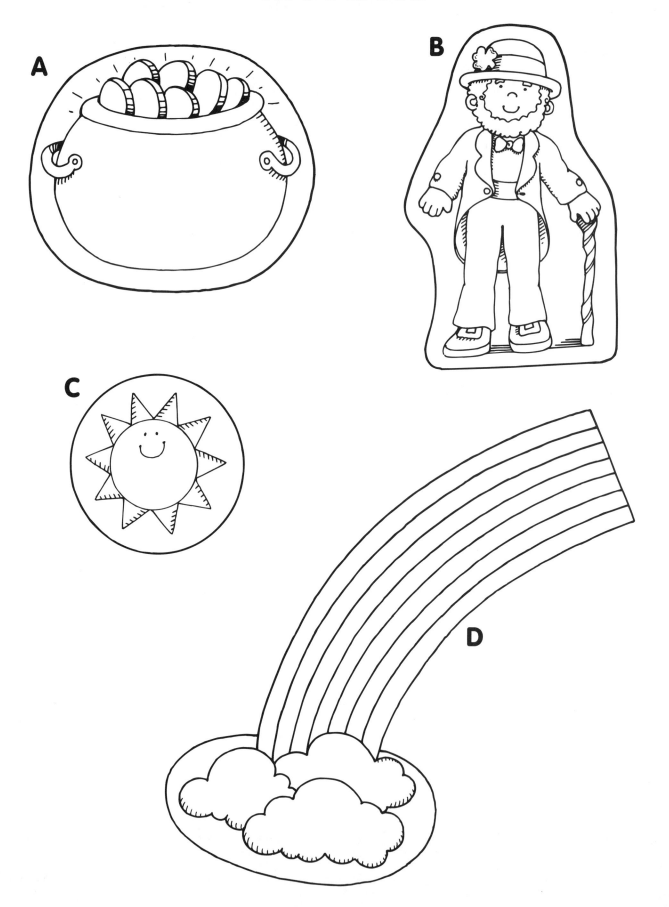

A

B

C

D

A little bit of blarney
and some shamrocks emerald green.

1

A giant pot of sparkling gold—
the brightest I've ever seen!

2

Layer It! Each Month © 2002 Creative Teaching Press

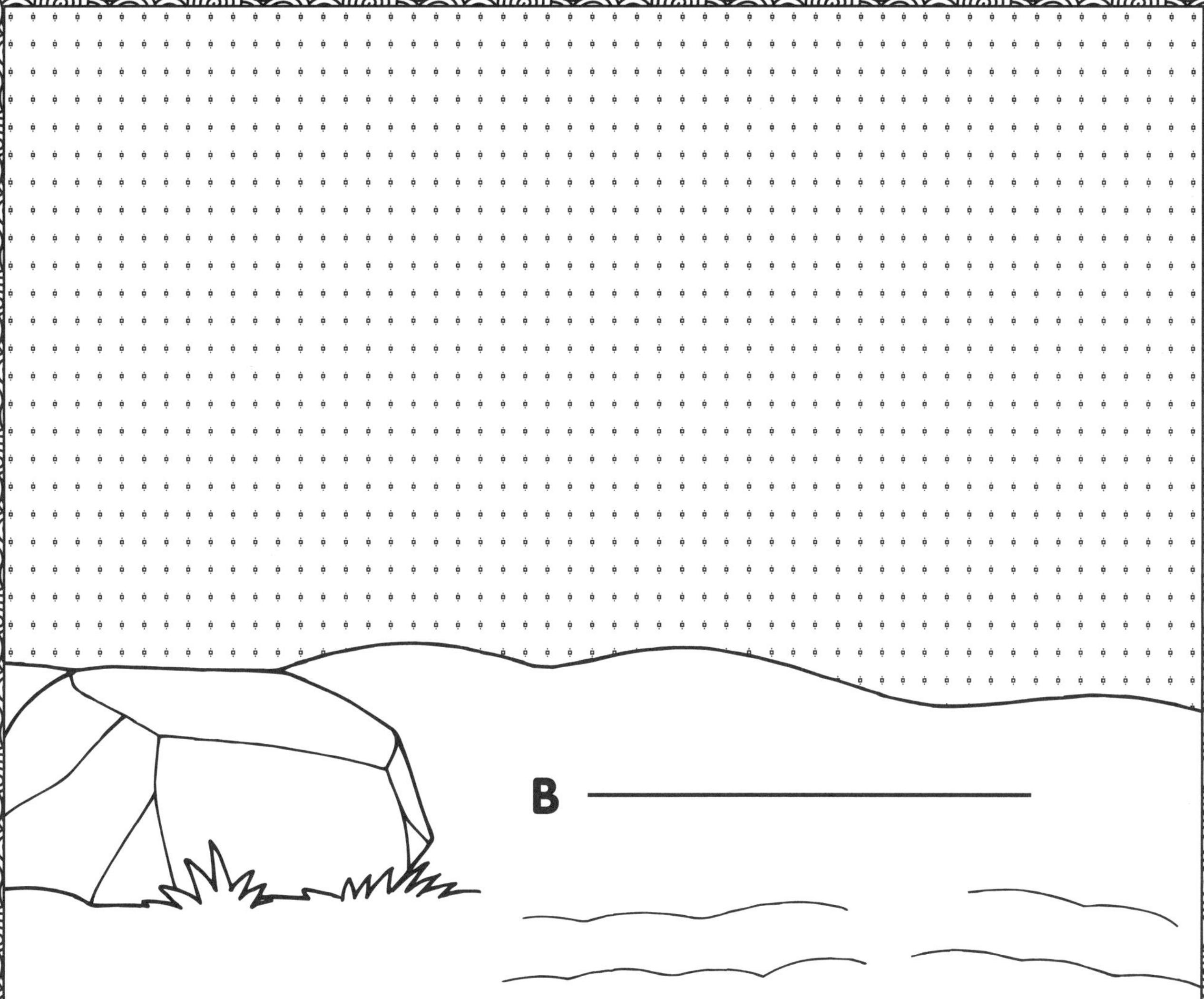

B _____

_____

I told my wish to a leprechaun
who loves to tease and play.

I wish for _____

_____

_____

3

C

D

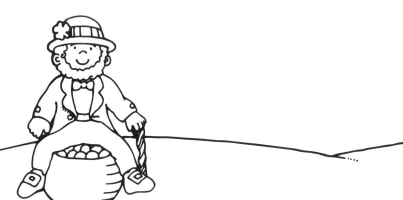

Look for him at the end of the rainbow
on this Saint Patrick's Day.

Happy Saint Patrick's Day!

4

Layer It! Each Month © 2002 Creative Teaching Press

April: Spring Has Sprung

Materials

- ✂ Art Pieces reproducible (page 52) white
- ✂ Page One reproducible (page 53) yellow
- ✂ Page Two reproducible (page 54) light green
- ✂ Page Three reproducible (page 55) green
- ✂ Page Four reproducible (page 56) pink
- ✂ crayons or markers
- ✂ scissors
- ✂ X-ACTO® knife (optional) (for teacher use only)
- ✂ craft sticks
- ✂ glue
- ✂ green glitter
- ✂ cotton balls

Directions •

Art Pieces Give each child an Art Pieces reproducible and an envelope. Have children color and cut out the nine art pieces and place them inside their envelope. Tell children to place their envelope in their file folder. Collect each child's folder, and distribute it at the beginning of each day's activity.

Page One Cut a slit next to the letter A on each child's Page One reproducible. Give children their revised page and a craft stick. Have them remove the worm and the rock art pieces from their envelope. Tell children to cut off the diamond pattern on the page and discard it. Ask them to color the remainder of the page. Have children glue the worm to the craft stick, glue the top edge of the rock over the letter B, and slide the prepared craft stick through the slit.

Page Two Give each child a Page Two reproducible and green glitter. Have children remove the two flower art pieces from their envelope. Tell children to cut off the diamond pattern on the page and discard it. Ask them to color the remainder of the page and glue glitter on the edge of the page to resemble grass. Set aside the pages until the glue is dry, and then have

children glue the flower art pieces over the letters C and D.

Page Three Give each child a Page Three reproducible. Have children remove the bird, squirrel, and cover art pieces from their envelope. Tell children to cut off the diamond pattern on the page and discard it. Ask them to color the remainder of the page and then glue the bird over the letter E and the squirrel over the letter F. Have children glue the top edge of the cover over the letter G (along the top edge of the tree hole).

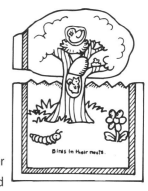

Page Four Give each child a Page Four reproducible and one cotton ball. Have children remove the boy and girl art pieces from their envelope. Ask children to color the page and then glue the boy over the letter H and the girl over the letter I. Invite them to respond to the writing prompt and tear their cotton ball into small pieces and glue the pieces on the cloud. Set aside the pages until the glue is dry.

Art Pieces

Layer It! Each Month © 2002 Creative Teaching Press

A _____

Worms in the garden.

B

1

C

D

Flowers in the grass.

2

Birds in their nests.

3

H

I

It's spring at last!

My favorite thing to do in the spring is _____

_____

_____

4

May: Marvelous Mom

Materials

- ✂ Art Pieces reproducible (page 58) white
- ✂ Page One reproducible (page 59) white
- ✂ Page Two reproducible (page 60) light green
- ✂ Page Three reproducible (page 61) light blue
- ✂ Page Four reproducible (page 62) yellow
- ✂ crayons or markers
- ✂ scissors
- ✂ X-ACTO® knife (optional) (for teacher use only)
- ✂ craft sticks
- ✂ glue

Directions •

Art Pieces
Give each child an Art Pieces reproducible and an envelope. Have children color and cut out the three art pieces and place them inside their envelope. Tell children to place their envelope in their file folder. Collect each child's folder, and distribute it at the beginning of each day's activity.

Page One
Give each child a Page One reproducible. Tell children to cut off the diamond pattern on the page and discard it. Ask them to color the remainder of the page.

Page Two
Cut a slit next to the letter A on each child's Page Two reproducible. Give children their revised page and a craft stick. Have children remove the mother art piece from their envelope and glue it to the craft stick. Tell them to cut off the diamond pattern on the page and discard it. Ask children to color the remainder of the page and then slide the prepared craft stick through the slit.

Page Three
Cut a slit below the letter B on each child's Page Three reproducible. Give children their revised page and a craft stick. Have children remove the child art piece from their envelope and glue it to the craft stick. Tell them to cut off the diamond pattern on the page and discard it. Ask children to color the remainder of the page and then slide the prepared craft stick through the slit.

Page Four
Give each child a Page Four reproducible. Have children remove the award art piece from their envelope. Ask children to color the page and draw in the picture frame a picture of themselves with their mother. Have them glue the top edge of the award over the letter C (along the top edge of the picture frame). Invite children to respond to the writing prompt.

Art Pieces

A

B

C

clean up toys
clean room
make bed
wash dishes

I like to help my mother
around the house each day.

1

A _____

She always does so much with me.
I'm grateful in every way.

2

Layer It! Each Month © 2002 Creative Teaching Press

B

I try to be the best I can
to show how much I care.

3

My mom is sweet, kind, and loving;
no other can compare.

I love you, Mom!

Mom, I love you because _____

_____

_____

4

June: Dandy Dad

Materials

- ✂ Art Pieces reproducible (page 64) white
- ✂ Page One reproducible (page 65) light blue
- ✂ Page Two reproducible (page 66) blue
- ✂ Page Three reproducible (page 67) light green
- ✂ Page Four reproducible (page 68) green
- ✂ crayons or markers
- ✂ scissors
- ✂ X-ACTO® knife (optional) (for teacher use only)
- ✂ craft sticks
- ✂ glue

Directions •

Art Pieces Give each child an Art Pieces reproducible and an envelope. Have children color and cut out the three art pieces and place them inside their envelope. Tell children to place their envelope in their file folder. Collect each child's folder, and distribute it at the beginning of each day's activity.

Page One Give each child a Page One reproducible. Tell children to cut off the diamond pattern on the page and discard it. Ask them to color the remainder of the page.

Page Two Cut a slit next to the letter A on each child's Page Two reproducible. Give children their revised page and a craft stick. Have them remove the father and child art piece from their envelope and glue it to the craft stick. Tell children to cut off the diamond pattern on the page and discard it. Ask them to color the remainder of the page and then slide the prepared craft stick through the slit.

Page Three Give each child a Page Three reproducible. Have children remove the large father art piece from their envelope. Tell children to cut off the diamond pattern on the page and discard it. Ask them to color the remainder of the page and glue the father over the letter B.

Page Four Give each child a Page Four reproducible. Have children remove the You're #1 art piece from their envelope. Ask children to color the page and draw in the frame a picture of themselves with their father. Have them glue the top edge of the sign over the letter C (along the top edge of the picture frame). Invite children to respond to the writing prompt.

Art Pieces

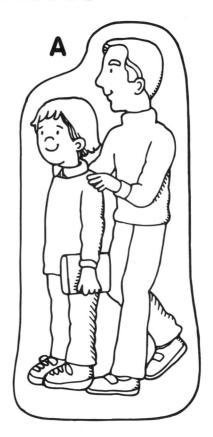

A

B

C

My dad's a really
special guy,
and I am glad
to tell you why.

1

A _____

When I work and when I play,
my dad is there to show me the way.

2

B

Time for me he can always find
because my dad is
thoughtful, caring, and kind.

3

He makes me proud,

and it's plain to see

that he will always be

important to me.

I love you, Dad!

Dad, I love you because _____

_____

_____

4

July: Patriotic Display

Materials

- ✄ Art Pieces reproducible (page 70) white
- ✄ Page One reproducible (page 71) red
- ✄ Page Two reproducible (page 72) white
- ✄ Page Three reproducible (page 73) blue
- ✄ Page Four reproducible (page 74) white
- ✄ crayons or markers
- ✄ scissors
- ✄ 1" (2.5 cm) scrap paper squares
- ✄ glue
- ✄ X-ACTO® knife (optional) (for teacher use only)
- ✄ craft sticks
- ✄ red glitter
- ✄ brass fasteners

Directions ●

Art Pieces Give each child an Art Pieces reproducible and an envelope. Have children color and cut out the three art pieces and place them inside their envelope. Tell children to place their envelope in their file folder. Collect each child's folder, and distribute it at the beginning of each day's activity.

Page One Give each child a Page One reproducible and a piece of scrap paper. Have children remove the Bill of Rights art piece from their envelope. Tell children to cut off the diamond pattern on the page and discard it. Have them fold their scrap paper "accordion style," glue the Bill of Rights onto one end of the folded paper, and glue the other end of the folded paper over the letter A. The art piece should "pop off" the page. Set aside the pages until the glue is dry.

Page Two Give each child a Page Two reproducible. Tell children to cut off the diamond pattern on the page and discard it. Ask them to color the remainder of the page.

Page Three Cut a slit next to the letter B on each child's Page Three reproducible. Give children their revised page and a craft stick. Have children remove the marching soldiers art piece from their envelope and glue it to the craft stick. Tell them to cut off the diamond pattern on the page and discard it. Ask children to color the remainder of the page and then slide the prepared craft stick through the slit.

Page Four Give each child a Page Four reproducible, red glitter, and a brass fastener. Have children remove the flag art piece from their envelope. Have them glue red glitter to the shaded stripes on the flag. Set aside the art pieces until the glue is dry. Invite children to respond to the writing prompt and then color the page. Tell them to place the brass fastener through the dot on the flag and the dot on the page (below the letter C).

Art Pieces

A

Bill of Rights

We the people…

B

C

A

Hooray!
for the rights
of all mankind.

1

Hooray! for integrity, too.

2

B _____

Hooray! for the service
of brave women and men.

3

c
●

Hooray! for the red, white, and blue.

This country is a good place to live because _____

_____

_____

4

August: Splash and Play

Materials

- ✄ Art Pieces reproducible (page 76) white
- ✄ Page One reproducible (page 77) yellow
- ✄ Page Two reproducible (page 78) light green
- ✄ Page Three reproducible (page 79) green
- ✄ Page Four reproducible (page 80) blue
- ✄ crayons or markers
- ✄ scissors
- ✄ green glitter
- ✄ glue
- ✄ X-ACTO® knife (optional) (for teacher use only)
- ✄ craft sticks

Directions •

Art Pieces Give each child an Art Pieces reproducible and an envelope. Have children color and cut out the six art pieces and place them inside their envelope. Tell children to place their envelope in their file folder. Collect each child's folder, and distribute it at the beginning of each day's activity.

Page One Give each child a Page One reproducible and green glitter. Have children remove the kids and water art pieces from their envelope. Tell them to cut off the diamond pattern on the page and discard it. Ask children to color the remainder of the page and glue the kids over the letter A. Have them glue the top edge of the water over the letter B (along the top edge of the pond). Invite children to glue glitter around the page to resemble grass. Set aside the pages until the glue is dry.

Page Two Cut a slit next to the letter C on each child's Page Two reproducible. Give children their revised page and a craft stick. Have children remove the bicycle art piece from their envelope and glue it to the craft stick. Tell them to cut off the diamond pattern on the page

and discard it. Ask children to color the remainder of the page and then slide the prepared craft stick through the slit.

Page Three Cut a slit next to the letter D on each child's Page Three reproducible. Give children their revised page and a craft stick. Have children remove the football art piece from their envelope and glue it to the craft stick. Tell them to cut off the diamond pattern on the page and discard it. Ask children to color the remainder of the page and then slide the prepared craft stick through the slit.

Page Four Cut a slit next to the letter F on each child's Page Four reproducible. Give children their revised page and a craft stick. Have children remove the sun and car art pieces from their envelope and glue the car to the craft stick. Ask them to color the page and glue the sun over the letter E. Invite children to respond to the writing prompt and then slide the prepared craft stick through the slit.

Art Pieces

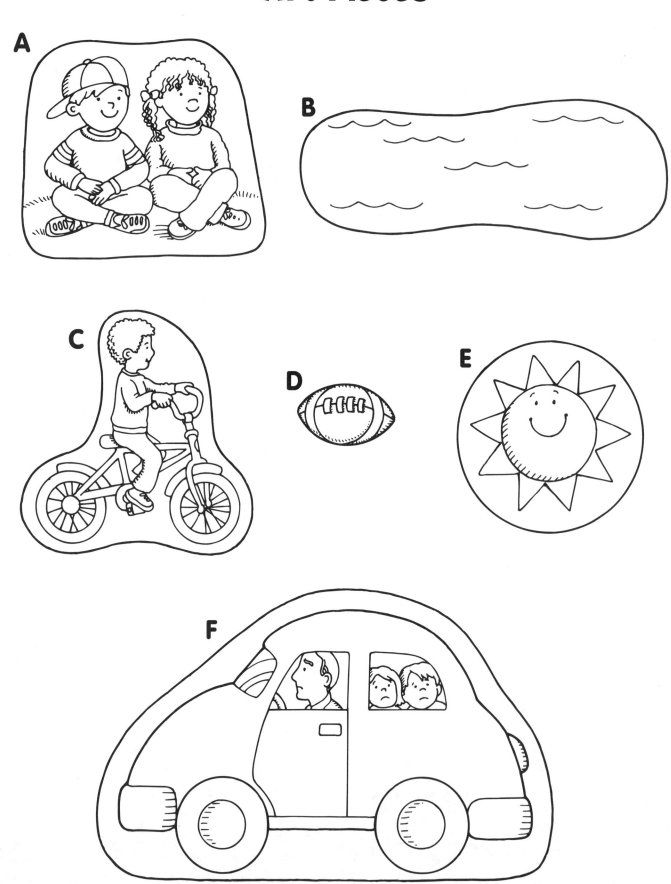

A

B

C

D

E

F

Layer It! Each Month © 2002 Creative Teaching Press

A

B

Summertime was lots of fun.

1

There was plenty to do for everyone.

2

We spent time together
and enjoyed the sun.

3

E

F

It was sad for us all
when vacation was done.

My favorite part of vacation was _____

_____

_____

4